P9-DTG-966

How to Be a Scientist

Analyze This!
Understanding the Scientific Method

Susan Glass

Heinemann Library
Chicago, Illinois

L.C.C. SOUTH CAMPUS LIBRARY

© 2007 Heinemann Library
a division of Reed Elsevier Inc.
Chicago, Illinois

Customer Service 888–454–2279

Visit our website at www.heinemannlibrary.com

All rights reserved. No part of this publication may be reproduced or transmitted in any form or by any means, electronic or mechanical, including photocopying, recording, taping, or any information storage and retrieval system, without permission in writing from the publisher.

Photo research by Ruth Blair and Ginny Stroud-Lewis
Designed by Victoria Bevan and AMR Design Ltd
Printed in China by WKT Company Ltd

11 10 09 08 07
10 9 8 7 6 5 4 3 2 1

Library of Congress Cataloging-in-Publication Data
Glass, Susan.
  Analyze this! : understanding the scientific method / Susan Glass.
    p. cm. -- (How to be a scientist)
  Includes bibliographical references and index.
  ISBN-13: 978-1-4034-8358-4 (library binding (hardcover))
  ISBN-10: 1-4034-8358-2 (library binding (hardcover))
  ISBN-13: 978-1-4034-8362-1 (pbk.)
  ISBN-10: 1-4034-8362-0 (pbk.)
  1. Science--Methodology--Juvenile literature. I. Title. II. Series: Glass, Susan. How to be a
    scientist.
  Q175.2.G57 2007
  507.2--dc22
  2006010638

Acknowledgments
The author and publisher are grateful to the following for permission to reproduce copyright material: Alamy Images pp. 38 (Chris Cameron), 42 (David Young-Wolff), 5 (Holt Studios International Ltd), 40 (Juniors Bildarchiv), 43 (Phil Degginger), 14 (Popperfoto); Corbis pp. 4, 8, 9, 12, 18, 26; Corbis/Bettmann, 6, 24; Corbis pp. 7 (David Samuel Robbins), 11 (Denis Scott), 27 (Karen Kasmauski), 28 (Owaki – Kulla), 41 (Shift Photo/zefa); Frank Lane Picture Agency p. 34 (S & D & K Maslowski); Getty Images pp. 15 (Hulton Archive), 10 (Photodisc); Harcourt Education pp. 34 (Ginny Stroud-Lewis), 33, 36, 36, 16, 21, 21, 21, 30, 39 (Tudor Photography); Mary Evans Picture Library pp. 13, 22; NASA p. 19; Photos.com p. 31; Science Photo Library pp. 23 (MARK THOMAS), 29 (NASA).

Cover photograph of a scientist wearing goggles in a laserlab reproduced with permission of Getty Images/Taxi

The publisher would like to thank Bronwen Howells for her assistance in the preparation of this book.

Dedication
I would like to thank my husband, John, for all his help and encouragement. I want to dedicate this book to him, my parents, my children Joanna, John, Billy, and Tricia, and my granddaughter Madison.

Q
175.2
.G57
2007

Every effort has been made to contact copyright holders of any material reproduced in this book. Any omissions will be rectified in subsequent printings if notice is given to the publisher.

Disclaimer
All the Internet addresses (URLs) given in this book were valid at the time of going to press. However, due to the dynamic nature of the Internet, some addresses may have changed, or sites may have changed or ceased to exist since publication. While the author and publishers regret any inconvenience this may cause readers, no responsibility for any such changes can be accepted by either the author or the publishers.

Contents

Some words are shown in bold, **like this**. You can find out what they mean by looking in the glossary.

Yellow Fever

During the Spanish–American War in Cuba in 1898, yellow fever killed thousands of American soldiers. The U.S. Army called in doctor–scientist Walter Reed and his team to stop this terrible disease.

Yellow fever was given its name because its victims turned yellow before they died. Many doctors and scientists believed it spread by contact with an infected person's clothes or bedding, but nobody knew for sure.

A scientist named Carlos Finlay thought mosquitoes were responsible for spreading the disease. He believed that when mosquitoes bit a sick person they could spread the disease by biting other people.

The investigation

Walter Reed started his scientific investigation with the question, "How is yellow fever spread?" Two possible answers were mosquitoes or contact with a sick person's clothes and bedding. He and his team set up two **experiments** to test these answers.

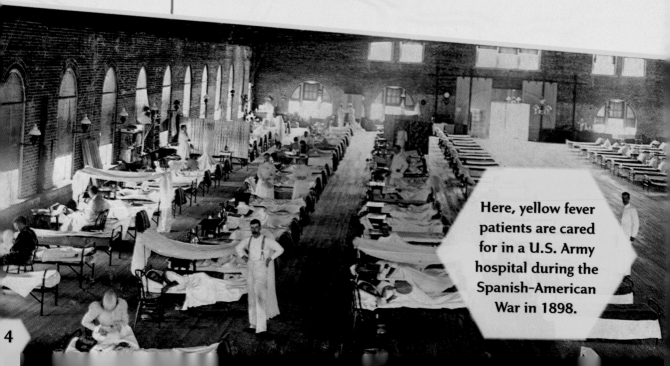

Here, yellow fever patients are cared for in a U.S. Army hospital during the Spanish–American War in 1898.

Mosquitoes can pass disease when they bite a healthy person after they have bitten a sick person.

Reed had two small houses built so that no mosquitoes could get in them. He had dirty bedding and clothes from yellow fever victims brought into one house. Three brave volunteers spent twenty days there, wearing the clothes and sleeping in the bedding. None of them got sick.

Reed and his team now knew that infected bedding was not the answer to the question. They then turned to mosquitoes. They let mosquitoes bite sick patients in the hospital. Then those same mosquitoes bit healthy volunteers who were staying in the other house. Some of the volunteers caught yellow fever. One doctor even died from the disease.

Science saves lives

The experiments proved that yellow fever is spread by mosquito bites. The U.S. Army launched a campaign to kill off mosquitoes. Killing the mosquitoes in the area stopped the spread of the disease. The scientific method and Reed's team saved the day!

DID YOU KNOW?

The doctors in Walter Reed's team experimented on people because no one knew of any animals that could get the disease. Some of Reed's team volunteered to be bitten. Most volunteers were soldiers. Their bravery saved thousands of lives.

Observe and ask questions

Scientists ask questions and find the answers in a careful, orderly way. Reed did not just try different ideas until one worked. He had a plan. First he decided which question he was trying to answer: "How is yellow fever spread?" He learned everything he could about the disease.

Form a hypothesis

Next Reed came up with possible answers, called **hypotheses**. Reed used the different ideas about how yellow fever spread as his hypotheses.

Plan an experiment

Reed's team needed to test their hypotheses. They designed an experiment to prove whether people caught yellow fever from infected blankets and clothing. They planned another experiment to see if people caught the disease from mosquitoes. They had special houses built in which to conduct their experiments.

Dr. Walter Reed had more than one hypothesis about yellow fever to test.

Yellow fever still exists in Africa, so mosquito nets are essential.

Conduct the experiment

During Reed's experiments, volunteers were kept away from other people. For the first experiment, mosquitoes were kept out of the house. That way, if the volunteers got sick, it was the bedding and clothes and not the moquitoes that caused it.

The second experiment was also controlled. Only mosquitoes that had bitten sick people were used. Other mosquitoes were kept out. Everything was kept very clean. The team tested several people. They did these things to make certain that it was the mosquitoes only that caused the disease.

Draw conclusions, communicate results

Reed's team wrote down details and kept careful records. Anyone who read them would understand the experiment. When the results showed that mosquitoes spread yellow fever, more testing was done on other volunteers to make certain.

Later it was learned that a **virus** actually causes the disease. The mosquitoes simply carry the virus from person to person.

DID YOU KNOW?

Mosquitoes breed in standing water. The army drained all **stagnant** bodies of water, or covered them with a layer of oil to kill the insects. Yellow fever had killed thousands of people in coastal cities in the United States. After Reed's discovery, yellow fever disappeared in the United States.

The Scientific Method

The word *science* comes from an old word, *scientia*, which means "to know." Science is a way to study the world around us. Science has been around for a long time, but new discoveries are still being made.

Science shapes the way we live today. The medicines we have, the cars and airplanes in which we travel, and the televisions and computers we use were all developed with the help of science. Even the food you eat and the clothes you wear are products of science.

A way of knowing

But what is science, exactly? Is it about mixing bubbling chemicals in test tubes? It can be, but it often is not. Science is a special way of finding the answers to questions. Scientists **investigate**, so doing scientific research is like being a detective. You get to solve mysteries. Even you can experiment with science at school and at home.

Space travel can happen because of scientific research.

Science has special steps that make up the **scientific method**. The word *method* means "an orderly way of doing something."

The scientific method has five steps:
1. Observe and ask questions
2. Form a hypothesis
3. Plan an experiment
4. Conduct the experiment
5. Draw conclusions and communicate results

Scientists do not always exactly follow this method. But Reed and his team used it to stop yellow fever. You can use it too.

TRY IT!

Around 800 years ago, people thought that rainbows were magical. A scientist called Roger Bacon did experiments to show they were not. He found that a rainbow in the air is the same as in a water spray. Rainbows occur when tiny droplets of water in the air bend and **reflect** light. If the sun is shining behind you, you can make your own rainbows by spraying water from a hose or spray bottle.

Observation

If you have a question you want answered, the scientific method can help. The first step in this process is research. Find out what has already been learned about the question you want answered. Chances are you are not the first person to ask it.

Scientists including Walter Reed build on the findings of other scientists. Like Walter Reed, you should complete your own careful **observation**. Observation means learning about things through your senses. Careful observation means looking at things in great detail.

Observation tools

Scientific tools and equipment let us observe things we otherwise could not. For example, **microscopes** help scientists observe worlds too tiny to see with eyes alone. Remote-controlled submarines explore the bottom of the ocean, acting as scientists' eyes, ears and hands there. **Telescopes** allow us to see far out into the universe.

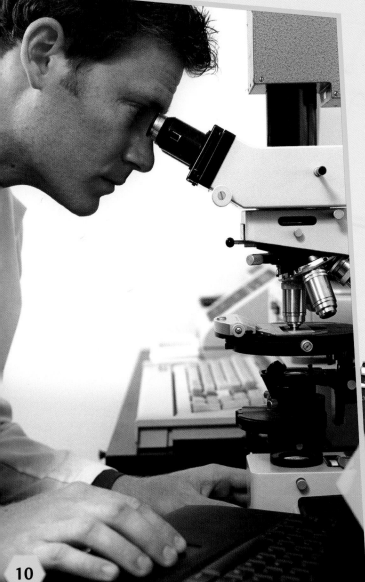

Scientists use high-tech microscopes to learn about tiny life forms.

The Hubble telescope circles Earth and sends us photographs, so that we can learn more about space.

DID YOU KNOW?

An observer on Earth has to look at the night sky through air. Clouds, dust, and moving air make it hard to see clearly far into space. Telescopes above the air have a better view. The Hubble Space Telescope (HST) was launched in 1990. It is a powerful tool for space observation. It circles Earth from 375 miles (600 kilometers) above it. The HST has sent home amazing images of star births, star deaths, and worlds far away.

Measurement

When scientists conduct experiments they often measure things. This helps them to observe more accurately. **Measurement** means finding the size or amount of something by comparing it to something else. We use tools such as rulers and scales to measure things.

Recording

Taking careful notes is another important part of the scientific method. This is called recording. Measurements should always be recorded. Writing down observations and details of your experiments lets others see what you have learned. Photographs, video, sound recordings, and computers are other ways to record observations. Recording also allows other people to repeat your experiments.

A Brief History of Science

People have always been curious about the world around them. When people in ancient times did not understand something they often thought it was magic or the work of gods. Eventually some people began to take a more logical approach. Math and **astronomy** were developed in the Middle East and China more than 4,000 years ago.

The Greeks

The ancient Greeks often thought like scientists. They asked serious questions about the world and tried to find practical answers. Aristotle lived more than 2,300 years ago. He used observation to find out for himself what was true.

Another Greek, Aristarchus of Samos, said that Earth moved around the Sun. He never tested this idea. Greek scientists did not always test things as scientists do now. Aristarchus's idea was not as popular as that of Ptolemy, another Greek. Ptolemy said the Sun and planets moved around Earth. His **theory** was believed for 1,400 years.

The ancient Greeks believed in observing and finding facts. They did some experiments. They built on the knowledge of earlier people, but believed in checking things for themselves.

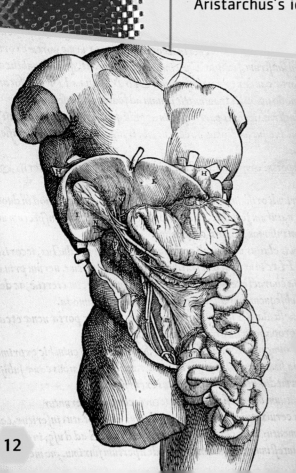

Vesalius was a Renaissance artist who studied dead bodies. In this way, he could make detailed sketches such as this one.

The Dark Ages

From about AD 400 to 900, Europe sank into the Dark Ages. During this period, European people did not learn many new things. During that time in the Middle East, Arabic scientists translated many of the old Greek books, which prevented the work of the ancient Greeks from being forgotten.

The Renaissance

Renaissance means "rebirth." This name was given to the time from about 1300 to 1527 when there was a rebirth of learning in Europe. In the 1400s a German printer named Johannes Gutenberg invented the printing press. As a result books could be printed quickly and ideas could be shared. Old and new knowledge spread.

DID YOU KNOW?

Sir Francis Bacon (1561–1626) helped develop the scientific method by teaching that scientists should experiment. It is thought that Bacon died after he caught a chill while doing an experiment. He wanted to see if stuffing a chicken with snow would keep it from rotting.

A new way

In the past scientists did not use the scientific method we use today. For example, Aristotle was a great thinker in ancient Greece. He carefully observed and tried to check things for himself. But he also wrote things down that had not been proven by the kind of careful experiments scientists complete today. Sometimes Aristotle was wrong. But his work was so respected in Europe that 1,000 years later few people doubted what he had written.

Until the 1500s **university** students were not supposed to question what Aristotle and other ancient thinkers had written. They were just supposed to memorize it. Experimenting and checking things were simply not done. But in the 1500s, things began to change. One man who made it change was Galileo Galilei.

As a student Galileo was taught that heavier objects fall faster than light ones. Aristotle had said this was true. After all, we have all noticed a feather falls slower than a rock. But Galileo decided not to accept this. He rolled balls of different weights down a ramp. He compared how long it took them to reach the bottom. He proved the great Aristotle wrong.

This is a statue of the ancient Greek philosopher Aristotle.

Falling objects

Galileo learned that all things fall at the same speed unless **air resistance** comes into play. Air resistance is the pressure of air pushing against something. If there is no air in the way, a feather and a heavy object fall at the same speed. Astronauts have demonstrated this on the Moon, where there is no air.

Legend says that Galileo dropped balls from the Leaning Tower of Pisa to prove his hypothesis.

TRY IT!

Hold up a piece of paper and let it fall. It falls slowly because of air resistance. Take the same piece of paper and crumple it into a small ball. Let go and observe how it falls faster. It falls faster because it has less air resistance.

Follow in Galileo's footsteps

You can try Galileo's experiment for yourself. Make sure to follow the steps in the scientific method.

1 **Observe and ask questions**

First, state the question you are trying to answer, "Does a heavy ball fall faster than a light one?" Then, think about your own observations. You have probably had experience with basketballs, tennis balls, playground balls, and others. Did the heavier ones seem to fall faster? Do research by looking up more information about Galileo's experiments.

2 **Form a hypothesis**

A hypothesis should be based on observation and research. Galileo's hypothesis stated that a heavy ball and a light one fall at the same speed. You can use this hypothesis too.

3 **Plan an experiment**

Galileo rolled balls down a ramp because he could time them better. He reasoned that rolling was like falling, only slower. He used wooden balls of different weights. You can drop different types of balls to see which falls faster.

Find balls that have different weights for your experiment.

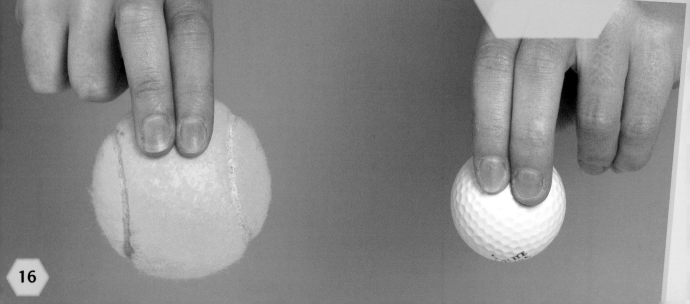

④ Conduct the experiment

Stand on a chair and drop two balls of different weights from upraised arms. Be careful to let go of both at the same time. Watch them land. You might need a partner to help you observe them landing. If possible try to use balls that are equally smooth on the outside. This might be difficult but it would make a better experiment.

Like Galileo you should repeat the test several times. Record the number of times the heavy ball landed first. Record the number of times the lighter one landed first. Record the number of times they landed together. A tally **graph** would be an easy way to keep track.

⑤ Draw conclusions and communicate results

After analyzing his results, Galileo concluded that his hypothesis was correct. A heavy ball and a light one fall at the same speed. Galileo shared his findings with other scientists. Do your results support the hypothesis? They should!

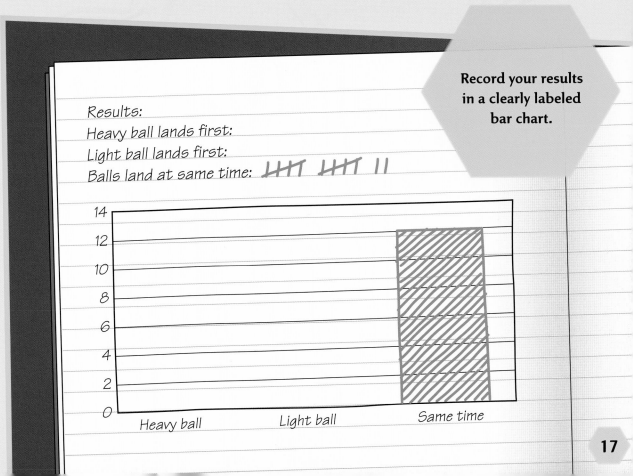

Record your results in a clearly labeled bar chart.

Results:
Heavy ball lands first:
Light ball lands first:
Balls land at same time: ⅢⅢ ⅢⅢ ‖

The first modern scientist

Galileo was one of the first scientists to use the scientific method we use today. When he wanted to find the answer to a question, he developed a hypothesis. Then he tested it with an experiment. He recorded his results and used them to prove or disprove his hypothesis. He tested things again to make sure his results were accurate. Many people consider him the first modern scientist.

Tools for observation

Galileo is also important because he improved observations by using tools. Galileo invented one of the first thermometers to measure temperature. But probably the most important science tool Galileo taught scientists to use was the telescope.

In 1608 a Dutch **lens** grinder put two lenses inside a tube. This was the first telescope. Galileo soon built a stronger telescope. He was the first person to use a telescope to study space.

Galileo Galilei helped to develop many scientific tools that are used today.

Pendulum clocks

Galileo was always asking questions. When he was a young man sitting in church he looked at a lamp hanging from the ceiling. It swung back and forth. Nobody had watches back then and clocks were not very accurate, so he used his **pulse** as a kind of stopwatch. He measured how long each swing took. As the lamp began to settle into place, the swings grew shorter. But he noticed it still took the same amount of time for each swing.

The lamp had acted like a **pendulum**. Galileo made pendulums with materials of different **masses** and different lengths of string. He tested the pendulums to find out as much as he could about how they worked.

Galileo was the first person to see the moons of Jupiter.

DID YOU KNOW?

Galileo used his telescope to discover the four largest moons of Jupiter. They are called the Galilean moons after him. Their names are Io, Europa, Ganymede, and Callisto.

Galileo's pendulum experiments

You can try Galileo's pendulum investigations to discover what changes the time of a pendulum's swing. You can use a stopwatch to time the swings.

1 **Observe and ask questions**

Your question can be the same one Galileo had 400 years ago: "How do you increase the number of swings a pendulum makes in fifteen seconds?"

2 **Form a hypothesis**

Think about the things that might make a pendulum swing faster. Perhaps changing the weight or length of the string will work, or changing the angle of release (height from which you drop the weight). These are three separate hypotheses. They can be tested in three separate experiments.

3 **Plan your experiments**

You can use a pendulum made from string and metal washers. Cut a length of string and tie a small loop at each end. Fit one loop over a pencil. Tape the pencil to a desktop or table with half of the pencil off the edge of the desk. Poke a paper clip through the loop at the other end. Use this to hang washers or other weights.

Now you have a pendulum. Try three different tests. In each test, only one **variable** should change. Everything else should stay the same.

4 **Conduct the experiments**

Work with a partner to conduct each of your three experiments. One partner can be the timer. The other partner can count the swings. Do not push the pendulum. Just let it go. After fifteen seconds, the timing partner can say, "Stop!" Record the number of swings.

1. Use different weights on the pendulum.
2. Release the pendulum from different angles.
3. Try different lengths of string.

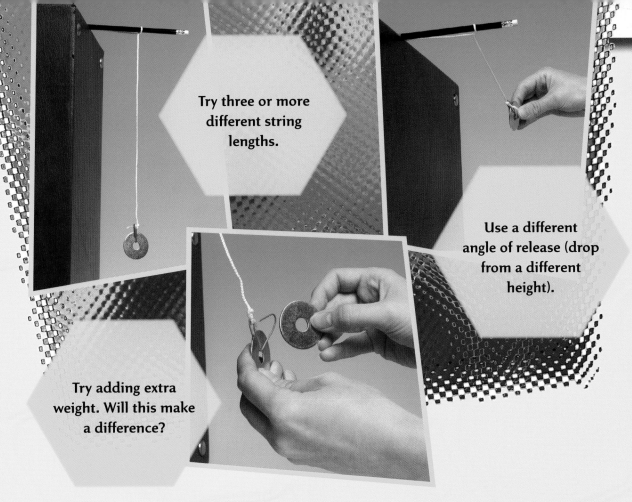

Try three or more different string lengths.

Use a different angle of release (drop from a different height).

Try adding extra weight. Will this make a difference?

⑤ Draw conclusions and communicate results
Put your results on a graph. They should show that shorter strings increase the swings your pendulum makes in fifteen seconds.

A pendulum is any weight that swings back and forth. As you collect your results, record them in tables.

Different weights:

Washers	Swings
1	12
2	12
3	12

Changing the weight does not change the number of swings.

Different angles:

Angle	Swings
high	12
medium	12
low	12

Changing the angle does not change the number of swings.

Different lengths:

Length	Swings
short	19
medium	12
long	9

Changing the length changes the number of swings.
A short pendulum swings faster.

Other Scientists, Other Methods

Not all scientists after Galileo followed the **fair test** method of completing experiments. Even so, some of them also moved science forward. In the 1600s Sir Isaac Newton explained how planets and moons move in space. He based much of his work on mathematics.

Another scientist in the 1600s, Anton van Leeuwenhoek (pronounced "lay-ven-hook"), discovered microbes with a homemade microscope. Microbes are microscopic living things. Van Leeuwenhoek was not following a fair test experiment, but he was recording and communicating careful observations.

Carolus Linnaeus helped advance science by setting up a **classification** system for plants and animals in the1700s. Linnaeus did not conduct experiments. Instead, he organized information so it could be understood better.

Edward Jenner

By the 1700s many people were using the scientific method. One of them was Edward Jenner, who lived in England at a time when smallpox was common. Smallpox was a dangerous disease. It killed many of its victims and left its survivors covered with scars.

Edward Jenner is shown vaccinating a young boy with cowpox.

People who milked cows often caught a disease called cowpox. Cowpox was milder than smallpox and less dangerous. Jenner heard farmers say that people who caught cowpox did not get smallpox. He decided to investigate and see if this was true.

Jenner put some liquid from a cowpox sore into a cut in a healthy boy's arm. The boy came down with a mild case of cowpox, but he recovered. Some weeks later Jenner gave the boy some liquid from a smallpox sore. The boy did not get smallpox. Jenner followed this with many more experiments and careful observation. Later, he published his results. Others started giving people cowpox this way to save them from smallpox.

The results of Jenner's work are still being used today. Babies are vaccinated to protect them against illness.

DID YOU KNOW?

Jenner's idea spread around the world. His treatment came to be called *vaccination*. It is based on the Latin word *vacca*, which means "cow," as in cowpox. People no longer get vaccinated for smallpox because Jenner's vaccine conquered the disease. But children today do receive vaccinations for other diseases such as measles, mumps, and rubella.

Gregor Mendel

Gregor Mendel lived in Austria in the 1800s. He researched **genetics**, the study of the passing of **traits** from parents to offspring. Traits are things like eye color and hair color that you get from your parents. In plants, a trait might be the color or shape of a flower, the size of a plant, or the juiciness of a fruit.

Mendel was a religious monk who looked after the monks' garden. They grew vegetables to eat, and he wanted to improve their crops. He wanted to know if there were patterns of traits being passed from parent plants to new plants. If Mendel could find these patterns, he could pick good traits and make them happen more often in new plants. That way, he could improve the crops. His hypothesis was that there were patterns of traits being passed down. He set out to find them.

Gregor Mendel did many experiments with pea plants.

DID YOU KNOW?

By choosing a trait that is useful and breeding more plants with that trait, scientists have been able to improve crops. Many more people can be fed because crops have been improved.

Pea plants

Over many years Mendel experimented with pea plants. Pea plants each have two parent plants. **Pollen** from one parent plant **fertilizes** the other plant. Then seeds for new plants are formed. Each parent passes on traits to the new plants.

Mendel carefully crossed tall plants with other tall ones, tall ones with short ones, and short ones with short ones. He measured the plants that grew from their seeds. He grew many generations to see how many became tall and short. He kept careful records. He studied around 28,000 pea plants!

Mendel's results showed there were patterns of traits being passed down from generation to generation. He learned that some traits were dominant. Dominant traits seem to overpower other traits. His hypothesis was correct. Plant growers and scientists could choose useful plant traits and breed plants with those traits.

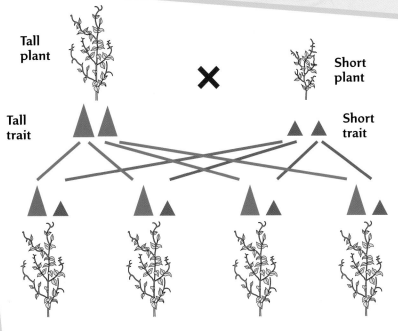

Tall plant
Short plant
Tall trait
Short trait

When tall pea plants are crossed with short ones, the offspring are tall.

All offspring are tall, proving that tall is the dominant trait.

Modern Science

During the past 300 years, science has made huge advances. The scientific method has brought us electricity, radios, telephones, movies, cars, planes, and spaceships. The scientific method helps to unlock the secrets of Earth and space.

Science is applied to almost every part of our lives. Telephones, computers, televisions, CDs, DVDs, medicines, and even clothing and food are all products of the scientific method.

A bright idea

As one example, just think of all the ways you use electricity. Take the light bulb. Around 120 years ago, people lit their houses with gas lamps. Before that, they used candles. Thomas Edison invented the light bulb. His question was, "How can we use electricity to provide light?" His hypothesis was that he could find a material that would glow but not burn out quickly if an electric current ran through it.

He experimented and experimented. He worked five long years testing hundreds of kinds of fibers. Finally, he found one that worked!

Seattle's city lights show Edison's invention at work.

Dolly the sheep was a famous genetic clone.

Cloning

Another example of the scientific method's impact on our lives can be found in genetics. One development in that field is cloning, the making of a new animal that is a copy of the parent. Scientists start cloning from a cell taken from the parent animal.

Animals are hard to clone. Scientists first tried cloning frogs in the 1950s. They have done countless experiments, using the scientific method to test many ways of cloning animals. They learned something from each experiment. Finally in 1996 scientists cloned a sheep named Dolly. They have also cloned mice, monkeys, pigs, and a cat.

TRY IT!

Plants have been cloned for hundreds of years. Cutting a piece from a plant and growing a new plant from it is cloning. You can clone a begonia or coleus plant. Cut some stem and a leaf off and plant it in some potting soil. If it grows, you have a genetic copy of the old plant—a clone.

Science improves lives

Scientific progress over the last century has been amazing. Scientists are working to understand our world—in space, under the sea, in deserts and rain forests, at volcanoes, and in labs. They are finding ways to save animals, fight diseases, feed the world's people, reduce **pollution**, and make the world a better place.

Scientists make our world safer by testing different car designs using crash dummies. They crash them over and over again to come up with the safest car designs. Scientists also use the scientific method to solve crimes. They use microscopes and genetic evidence to help them catch criminals.

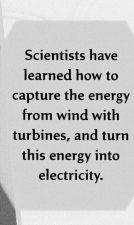

Scientists have learned how to capture the energy from wind with turbines, and turn this energy into electricity.

DID YOU KNOW?

Some scientists dream of bringing back animal species that are **extinct**. They have collected genetic material from a woolly mammoth found frozen in the ice in Siberia. Mammoths became extinct around 10,000 years ago. There is hope that scientists will be able to grow a cloned mammoth someday.

Finding cleaner energy sources

The scientific method is used to come up with clean, safe ways to power our cars and heat and light our homes. One possible solution scientists are testing is hydrogen-powered cars. If cars run on hydrogen instead of gas, they do not dirty the air. The only thing that comes out of the exhaust pipe is a small amount of water.

The scientific method is used every day to solve the world's problems. Scientists are testing better ways to use wind and ocean waves and sunlight to make electricity. These new methods are clean. We will never run out of wind, waves, and sunlight.

The scientific method is even used in space to find out about the effects of weightlessness, and to test the soil on Mars.

Testing Things Out

Professional scientists use the scientific method every day. You can use it too. Ask questions and make observations. Find out what others have already learned. Then make a hypothesis. Design an experiment to test it. Control the variables to make sure only one thing causes the results. Take notes and keep careful records. Measure things. Find out if your results prove your hypothesis. Share your findings. Think up new questions, hypotheses, and experiments. That is the scientific way of learning.

Do you already use it?

You may already use the scientific method without realizing it. For example, you may ask yourself, "Why isn't the remote control working?" You make a mental hypothesis and test it. Are the batteries dead? You take them out and try new ones. Still not fixed? Maybe the television is unplugged. You check on that. You test hypotheses one by one until you find the answer.

If something is not working, you need to form hypotheses and test them one by one to discover the reason for the problem.

Using the scientific method

You can use the scientific method to make your own life better. Can you change your morning routine to get ready for school in less time?

Remember the steps in the scientific method. First, observe and ask questions. Do you spend a long time using the hair dryer? Could you shorten that time by air-drying your hair while you eat breakfast, then finishing it with the dryer? Make hypotheses. Plan and conduct experiments. Write down how long it takes to do things in a different order or in different ways. Make sure you repeat each experiment more than once. Record your results. See if your results support your hypothesis. Then draw conclusions and communicate your results.

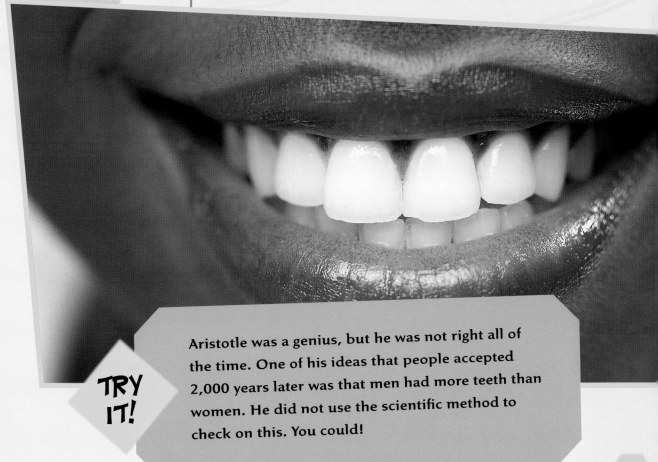

TRY IT!

Aristotle was a genius, but he was not right all of the time. One of his ideas that people accepted 2,000 years later was that men had more teeth than women. He did not use the scientific method to check on this. You could!

Plants and music

You do not have to be a professional scientist to use the scientific method. You too can ask questions about the world around you. Say your question is, "Do plants grow taller if they are exposed to music?"

1 Observe and ask questions

To answer this question, you would need to read about plants. You would need to know about how plants grow. You would try to find information on music's effect on plant growth.

2 Form a hypothesis

Light can affect a plant's growth. Say you decide that sound can affect a plant's growth too. Your hypothesis is that music will make the plants grow taller.

3 Plan an experiment

Plan your experiment so you can be sure what caused the outcome. A variable is anything that might affect the results of an experiment. Test only one variable. This means that everything should be the same for the plants except the music.

Think of everything that could affect the growth of plants. All the plants must get the same water, sunlight, and soil. Even the pots used for planting must be the same. Use the same type of plant. Controlling all the variables is the only way that you can be sure that if the plants grow differently that it was the music that caused it.

Finally, you would need to test lots of plants. If only one plant gets used and it grew badly or died, there would be no way of being sure why this had happened.

Measure the plants carefully and record the figures.

Conduct the experiment
Only one variable, the music, is left to determine how things turn out. Some of the plants should get music, and some should not. You should probably stick to one kind of music too, in case it makes a difference. Check the plants regularly and measure their growth. This experiment might take weeks to show results.

⑤ Draw conclusions and communicate results
Use the measurements to help decide if the hypothesis was proven correct. Display your results on a graph or chart for others to see.

We need measurements because sometimes our eyes and minds fool us. Measure the lines with a ruler. Is one longer?

33

Birds and birdseed

When you choose a question to investigate, make it one that you can prove an answer to. Say you enjoy having birds in your yard. You plan to feed them and want to know what kind of birdseed the birds like best.

1 **Observe and ask questions**
First find out all you can about the wild birds that visit your yard. Try the Internet, the library, and asking anyone who might know. Learn what you can about the available seed mixes for wild birds. Then go to the store and pick out two or three brands of birdseed. Read the information on the containers.

2 **Form a hypothesis**
Which birdseed do you think they will like best? Your hypothesis should be based on information. It should not be a wild guess. Your hypothesis might be that they prefer Brand B. This is something you could prove or disprove. It is a statement you can test.

Find the best birdseed to attract wild birds.

3 **Plan an experiment**
Plan an experiment to prove your hypothesis right or wrong. Make it a controlled experiment. To do so, keep everything the same except for the brand of birdseed. Any other variable that could affect the outcome must be the same for it to be a fair test.

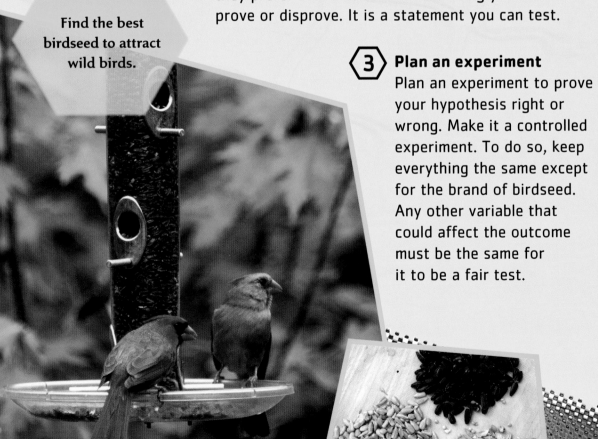

4 Conduct the experiment

Use measurements. You could weigh the birdseed or measure it another way. Put equal amounts out in the morning and measure what is left at night. Subtract to find out how much they ate. Keep records. Photographs and video would be useful, as well as written records. Repeat the experiment for several days.

5 Draw conclusions and communicate results

After you analyze your results, your conclusion might be that your hypothesis was proven correct. Or maybe it was proven incorrect. You may decide that more testing or better testing is needed. Then, if you are being a good scientist, let others know about your findings so they can copy your experiment.

Which brand do the birds like best? Have they liked this brand best throughout the experiment?

Results: Amount of birdseed eaten (in grams)

	Brand A	Brand B	Brand C
Day 1	120	95	110
Day 2	160	150	180
Day 3	115	105	110
Day 4	140	70	90

Fast reflexes

You notice that some of your friends have faster reflexes than others. You wonder if they were just born that way or if practice has made their reflexes faster.

① Observe and ask questions

You ask questions such as, "Does practice make a person react more quickly when trying to catch a ruler?" Do you think that people will react more quickly with practice? You could research it.

② Form a hypothesis

Say your hypothesis is, "Reaction time in catching a falling ruler will improve with practice."

③ Plan an experiment

You need to think of a way to time a person's reactions. You decide to drop a ruler for someone to catch. The markings on the ruler will show you how quickly they caught it. By making several drops, you can see if reaction time improves. You would need to test several people to see if the results are the same for everyone.

Record the centimeter number under the hand that catches the ruler.

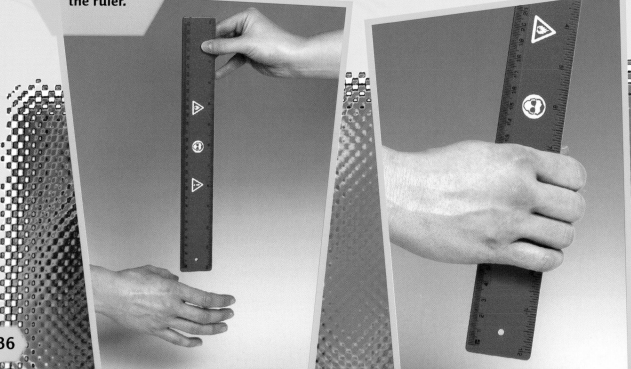

TOP TIP

In school you are used to having right and wrong answers to questions. But in science, it is fine if your hypothesis was wrong. You have not failed. You have still learned something.

4 Conduct the experiment

Stand up and hold a ruler by the end that says 30 cm. You must hold it at the same height each time. The person you are testing sits and holds his or her catching hand at the same height each time. You drop the ruler without warning. The person tries to grab it as quickly as possible. Record the centimeter marking where the hand catches the ruler. Drop and catch this way several times. Then test someone else. Write down the measurements for all the testers.

5 Draw conclusions and communicate results

Make a graph of the numbers for each person you tested. Was your hypothesis correct? Can you think of ways to improve the test? Do you have more questions to answer? For example, if practice improves reaction time for catching a ruler, does it mean that practice will also improve other reflexes?

Lots of tests may be needed to get clear results.

Results (in centimeters):

Tester	1st attempt	2nd attempt	3rd attempt
1	27	15	5
2	18	16	14
3	17	26	1
4	20	3	28
5	20	18	9

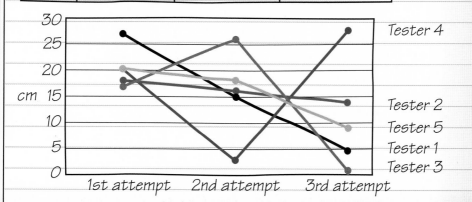

Floating boats

Have you ever wondered why a boat floats? Is it because it is made of material that floats?

1 Observe and ask questions

You may have observed that some boats are made of wood and you know that wood floats. But you have also seen ships made of steel. You have observed that most steel objects sink. So what makes a boat float?

2 Form a hypothesis

Because you have noticed that boats all have a similar shape, you hypothesize that the shape of a boat makes it float.

3 + 4 Plan and conduct an experiment

You decide to choose a material and test several different shapes. Fill a bowl with water. Drop a lump of modeling clay in the water. It sinks. Try shaping the clay in different ways to see if it will float. Repeat to be certain. Record your results for each shape.

Even huge metal ships can float. How is this possible?

Test a boat shape, a ball, and other shapes.

⑤ Draw conclusions and communicate results

You discover that clay formed into a boat shape floats, and so does a bowl shape. Other shapes and lumps all sink. Based on your results, you conclude that it is the shape of a boat that makes it float. You write up your results and display them on a chart.

You have answered your question but you decide to do further research about buoyancy. Buoyancy is an upward push on an object when it is in water. You have noticed that people seem to be lighter in water.

Buoyancy depends on how **dense** an object is. If two things are the same size, the one that weighs more is denser. If an object is denser than water, it sinks. A piece of clay is heavier than the amount of water that takes up the same space. But if you shape it like a boat, it is lighter. This is because the inside of a boat or ship is full of air. It is the same amount of clay, but it fills a larger space because it is hollow. The boat shape and the air in it together weigh less than the same volume of water. So a boat-shaped object floats, even if it is made of steel.

Other investigations

By now you have learned enough about the scientific method that you should be able to design your own experiments. What else could you investigate?

1 Observe and ask questions

Say you are right-handed and your brother is left-handed. You ask if your cat is right- or left-pawed. You would start the scientific method by observing cats and reading about them.

2 Form a hypothesis

Say that you could not find out much by observation and research, but you know most people are right-handed. You hypothesize that most cats will be too.

3 + 4 Plan and conduct an experiment

You decide to see which paw a cat uses to bat at a toy. Think about how it will work. How many cats should you test? Should you test each cat more than once? What variables need to be controlled?

5 Draw conclusions and communicate results

Did the results show a pattern? Was your hypothesis proven correct? Even if it was not, you have still learned something scientifically. It may lead you to do further research or experiments.

1. Observe and ask questions

Which gum's flavor lasts longest? Some gum's flavor seems to last longer. Some brands claim theirs lasts. Can you investigate and find out?

2. Form a hypothesis

Make your hypothesis based on advertising claims. Say you choose Brand X because its advertising claims that it has long-lasting flavor.

3 + 4. Plan and conduct an experiment

You decide to test two kinds of gum, Brand X and Brand Y. You will need people who can time each other. How will you decide when the flavor runs out? Should the same people test both types of gum? Should the testers know which type of gum they are chewing?

5. Draw conclusions and communicate results

Display the results on a chart. Which brand's flavor lasted longer? Do the results support your hypothesis? Is there anything you could change to make the experiment better?

> **Design your own experiments. What questions do you want to answer?**

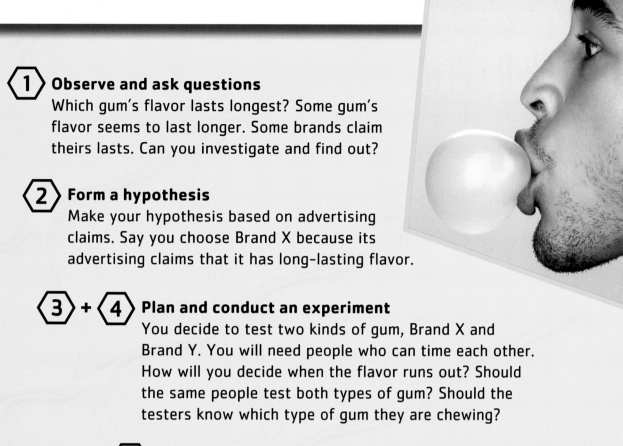

Which brand's flavor lasts longer?
Brand X: | | | |
Brand Y: |||| |||| |||| |||
Both the same: | |

Same 2

Brand X 4

Brand Y 15

Moving Forward

Science is a way to learn about the world. The scientific method is a way to find the answers to questions. Now that you have read this book, you should have a pretty good understanding of the scientific method and be able to use it.

You can read books to learn about animals, the stars, rocks, and anything else your curiosity leads you to. What do you find interesting? One famous fossil expert loved finding fossils and learning about dinosaurs as a kid. He never grew out of it. Now he makes a living digging up dinosaur bones.

Science careers

There are several branches of science you could learn more about. Many different jobs exist in all these branches. The scientific method is useful in all of them. Lots of other careers are not in the science field, but they use the scientific method.

Are you interested in the stars and planets? There is still much to learn in the field of astronomy. Did you know that new comets are still being discovered? Astronauts are scientists too.

Where will your curiosity lead you?

There are many different types of scientists. You could become one yourself.

Maybe you are interested in volcanoes and earthquakes. New things are being learned about the planet beneath our feet every year. Many exciting things are happening in plant and animal science. Researchers are developing new plants to feed the world's hungry people. There are many careers in medicine.

Science in everyday life

You can also use the scientific method in your everyday life. It is a wonderful way to solve problems and learn about the world. Let your curiosity be your guide. That is how to be a scientist!

TOP TIP

Every library has a science book section. Look in the nonfiction part of the library. Libraries organize nonfiction books by numbers. The 500–600 section includes science books.

Scientific Method Flowchart

OBSERVE AND ASK QUESTIONS

OBSERVE carefully. Do research. Think of a QUESTION you could answer by experimenting.

FORM A HYPOTHESIS

The HYPOTHESIS is what you think is the answer. It should be based on information. It is a statement that you can test.

PLAN AN EXPERIMENT

The EXPERIMENT is the way you test a hypothesis. The variables, all the things that could affect how it turns out, should be kept the same except for the one thing you are testing. Measurements should be made and recorded. Counting things is a way of measuring. Test things more than once.

CONDUCT THE EXPERIMENT

Follow your plan. Carefully observe and keep good records of your experiment. The results should be recorded in a way that makes it easy for others to understand.

DRAW CONCLUSIONS AND COMMUNICATE RESULTS

The CONCLUSION is where you decide if your RESULTS support your hypothesis or disprove it. Your experiment was successful either way. You learned something. Charts and graphs are good ways to communicate your results to others. If you kept good records, others can replicate, or copy, your experiment.

Timeline of Discovery

2500 to 500 BC Astronomy begins in China and the Middle East.

500 BC to AD 500 Ancient Greeks ask questions and think things happened due to natural causes, not the gods. They separate science from superstition.

AD 500 to 1500 Arabic people in the Middle East preserve the science of the ancient Greeks. The Dark Ages occur in Europe and not much progresses there at this time.

1500 to 1700 The Renaissance ("rebirth" of knowledge in Europe) and the Scientific Revolution continues. The printing press spreads knowledge. Galileo uses the modern scientific method in the late 1500s and early 1600s. Galileo does pendulum experiments in the 1580s. The telescope and microscope are invented. Sir Isaac Newton uses math to explain how objects move in space and on Earth. Van Leeuwenhoek discovers living things with his microscope.

1700 to 1800 Experimentation occurs in many areas. Linnaeus organizes a classifying system used to group plants and animals. Jenner experiments with smallpox vaccine.

1800 to 1900 Mendel studies inheritance in plants. Edison perfects the electric light bulb in 1879. Walter Reed controls yellow fever in 1901.

1900 to present Astronomers study the universe. Spacecraft explore the solar system. Cloning is advanced. Medicine makes huge strides. Computers, television, radio, and robots are developed. Scientists study clean energy sources such as hydrogen.

Glossary

air resistance pressure of air pushing against something

astronomy study of planets, stars, moons, and other things in space

classification grouping of things by how they are alike

dense heavier than another object of the same size

experiment careful test to see if a hypothesis is correct

extinct having all died out

fair test changing one thing at a time in an experiment while keeping everything else the same

fertilize to make a female plant or animal able to create offspring, seeds, or fruit

genetics study of heredity, the passing of traits from parents to offspring

graph diagram that shows the relationship between numbers

hypothesis (more than one are called hypotheses) answer to a question that can be tested by doing an experiment

investigate use the scientific method to learn something

lens piece of clear material curved on one or both sides to bend light passing through it

mass measurement of the amount of matter contained in an object

measurement finding the size or amount of something by comparing it to something else

microscope device that makes tiny things look larger, usually by using lenses

observation learning with your senses, especially by seeing

pendulum hanging weight that can swing freely back and forth

pollen part of male plant that fertilizes female plants

pollution harmful chemicals or waste in the water or air

pulse beat of blood through the body caused by the beating of the heart

reflect to bounce light off an object

scientific method scientific way of finding things out, usually following these steps: observation, asking questions, forming a hypothesis, planning and conducting experiments, drawing conclusions, and sharing results

stagnant not flowing, foul from standing still

telescope instrument that makes faraway objects look larger

theory explanation of how or why something happens, based on scientific study

trait qualities that a plant or animal gets from its parents

university school of higher education

vaccine shot or something swallowed that contains dead or weakened germs to protect against a disease

variable something that can be changed in an experiment

virus extremely tiny thing that can cause disease

Further Reading

Farndon, John. *Buoyancy*. Tarrytown, NY: Marshall Cavendish, 2002

Lafferty, Peter. *Forces and Motion*. Chicago: Raintree, 2001

Mason, Paul. *Galileo*. Chicago: Heinemann Library, 2001

Parker, Steve. *The Science of Forces*. Chicago: Heinemann Library, 2005

Index